FIRST
CORINTHIANS

Little Rock Scripture Study Staff

LITTLE ROCK SCRIPTURE STUDY

A ministry of the Diocese of Little Rock
in partnership with Liturgical Press

Dear Friends in Christ,

   The Bible comes to us as both a gift and an opportunity. It is a gift of God who loves us enough to communicate with us. The only way to enjoy the gift is to open and savor it. The Bible is also an opportunity to actually meet God who is present in the stories, teachings, people, and prayers that fill its pages.

   I encourage you to open your Bibles in anticipation that God will do something good in your life. I encourage you to take advantage of the opportunity to meet God in prayer, study, and small-group discussion.

   Little Rock Scripture Study offers materials that are simple to use, and a method that has been tested by time. The questions in this study guide will direct your study, help you to understand the passages you are reading, and challenge you to relate the Scriptures to your own life experiences.

   Allow the Word of God to form you as a disciple of the Lord Jesus. Accept the challenge to be "transformed by the renewal of your mind" (Romans 12:2). Above all, receive God's Word as his gift, and act upon it.

Sincerely in Christ,

✠ J. Peter Sartain
Bishop of Little Rock

Sacred Scripture

"The Church has always venerated the divine Scriptures just as she venerates the body of the Lord, since from the table of both the word of God and of the body of Christ she unceasingly receives and offers to the faithful the bread of life, especially in the sacred liturgy. She has always regarded the Scriptures together with sacred tradition as the supreme rule of faith, and will ever do so. For, inspired by God and committed once and for all to writing, they impart the word of God Himself without change, and make the voice of the Holy Spirit resound in the words of the prophets and apostles. Therefore, like the Christian religion itself, all the preaching of the Church must be nourished and ruled by sacred Scripture. For in the sacred books, the Father who is in heaven meets His children with great love and speaks with them; and the force and power in the word of God is so great that it remains the support and energy of the Church, the strength of faith for her sons, the food of the soul, the pure and perennial source of spiritual life."

Vatican II, Dogmatic Constitution on Divine Revelation, no. 21.

INTERPRETATION OF SACRED SCRIPTURE

"Since God speaks in sacred Scripture through men in human fashion, the interpreter of sacred Scripture, in order to see clearly what God wanted to communicate to us, should carefully investigate what meaning the sacred writers really intended, and what God wanted to manifest by means of their words.

"Those who search out the intention of the sacred writers must, among other things, have regard for 'literary forms.' For truth is proposed and expressed in a variety of ways, depending on whether a text is history of one kind or another, or whether its form is that of prophecy, poetry, or some other type of speech. The interpreter must investigate what meaning the sacred writer intended to express and actually expressed in particular circumstances as he used contemporary literary forms in accordance with the situation of his own time and culture. For the correct understanding of what the sacred author wanted to assert, due attention must be paid to the customary and characteristic styles of perceiving, speaking, and narrating which prevailed at the time of the sacred writer, and to the customs men normally followed in that period in their everyday dealings with one another."

Vatican II, Dogmatic Constitution on Divine Revelation, no. 12.

Instructions

MATERIALS FOR THE STUDY

This Study Guide: First Corinthians

Bible: The New American Bible with Revised New Testament or The New Jerusalem Bible is recommended. Paraphrased editions are discouraged as they offer little if any help when facing difficult textual questions. Choose a Bible you feel free to write in or underline.

Commentary: The New Collegeville Bible Commentary, volume 7, *First and Second Corinthians* by Maria A. Pascuzzi (Liturgical Press) is used with this study. The abbreviation for this commentary, NCBC-NT volume 7, and the assigned pages are found at the beginning of each lesson.

ADDITIONAL MATERIALS

Bible Dictionary: *The Dictionary of the Bible* by John L. McKenzie (Simon & Schuster) is highly recommended as a reference.

Notebook: A notebook may be used for lecture notes and your personal reflections.

WEEKLY LESSONS

Lesson 1—1 Cor 1–2
Lesson 2—1 Cor 3–4
Lesson 3—1 Cor 5–6
Lesson 4—1 Cor 7–8

Lesson 5—1 Cor 9–10
Lesson 6—1 Cor 11–12
Lesson 7—1 Cor 13–14:25
Lesson 8—1 Cor 14:26–15:34
Lesson 9—1 Cor 15:35–16:24

YOUR DAILY PERSONAL STUDY

The first step is prayer. Open your heart and mind to God. Reading Scripture is an opportunity to listen to God who loves you. Pray that the same Holy Spirit who guided the formation of Scripture will inspire you to correctly understand what you read and empower you to make what you read a part of your life.

The next step is commitment. Daily spiritual food is as necessary as food for the body. This study is divided into daily units. Schedule a regular time and place for your study, as free from distractions as possible. Allow about twenty minutes a day. Make it a daily appointment with God.

As you begin each lesson read the assigned chapters of Scripture found at the beginning of each lesson, the footnotes in your Bible, and then the indicated pages of the commentary. This preparation will give you an overview of the entire lesson and help you to appreciate the context of individual passages.

As you reflect on Scripture, ask yourself these four questions:

1. *What does the Scripture passage say?*
   Read the passage slowly and reflectively. Use your imagination to picture the scene or enter into it.

2. *What does the Scripture passage mean?*
   Read the footnotes and the commentary to help you understand what the sacred writers intended and what God wanted to communicate by means of their words.

3. *What does the Scripture passage mean to me?*
   Meditate on the passage. God's Word is living and powerful. What is God saying to you today? How does the Scripture passage apply to your life today?

4. *What am I going to do about it?*
   Try to discover how God may be challenging you in this passage. An encounter with God contains a challenge to know God's will and follow it more closely in daily life.

THE QUESTIONS ASSIGNED FOR EACH DAY

Read the questions and references for each day. The questions are designed to help you listen to God's Word and to prepare you for the weekly small-group discussion.

Some of the questions can be answered briefly and objectively by referring to the Bible references and the commentary *(What does the passage say?)*. Some will lead you to a better understanding of how the Scriptures apply to the Church, sacraments, and society *(What does the passage mean?)*. Some questions will invite you to consider how God's Word challenges or supports you in your relationships with God and others *(What does the passage mean to me?)*. Finally, the questions will lead you to examine your actions in light of Scripture *(What am I going to do about it?)*.

Write your responses in this study guide or in a notebook to help you clarify and organize your thoughts and feelings.

THE WEEKLY SMALL-GROUP MEETING

The weekly small-group sharing is the heart of the Little Rock Scripture Study Program. Participants gather in small groups to share the results of praying, reading, and reflecting on Scripture and on the assigned questions. The goal of the discussion is for group members to be strengthened and nourished individually and as a community through sharing how God's Word speaks to them and affects their daily lives. The daily study questions will guide the discussion; it is not necessary to discuss all the questions.

All members share the responsibility of creating an atmosphere of loving support and trust in the group by respecting the opinions and experiences of others, and by affirming and encouraging one another. The simple shared prayer which begins and ends each small group meeting also helps create the open and trusting environment in which group members can share their faith deeply and grow in the study of God's Word.

A distinctive feature of this program is its emphasis on and trust in God's presence working in and through each member. Sharing responses to God's presence in the Word and in others can bring about remarkable growth and transformation.

THE WRAP-UP LECTURE

The lecture is designed to develop and clarify the themes of each lesson. It is not intended to be the focus of the group's discussion. For this reason, the lecture always occurs *after* the small group discussion. If several small groups meet at one time, the groups may gather in a central location to listen to the lecture.

Lectures may be presented by a local speaker. They are also available in audio form on CD, and in visual form on cassette or DVD.

I Corinthians 1–2

NCBC-NT VOLUME 7, PAGES 5–28

Day I

1. Recall some blessings that have come into your life through previous reading and study of the Bible.

2. Write some of what you already know about First Corinthians, including favorite and/or confusing passages, or those of special interest to you.

3. Briefly describe the city of Corinth: its history, diverse population, commercial and social importance.

Day 2

4. What does verse 1 tell us about how Paul understands himself, his call and his function? (See Gal 1:1, 15.)

5. a) How does Paul use the term "ekklesia"(1:2) differently than it was used in the wider culture of the time?

   b) Do Paul's qualifications for the church (1:2) apply only to the church in Corinth?

6. What are some of the signs of God's faithfulness (1:9) that you notice on a regular basis?

Day 3

7. a) List some of the causes for rivalries among the Corinthians (1:10-13).

   b) Why are factions contrary to the Gospel (1:10-13)? (See John 17:21-23; Acts 4:32; Phil 2:1-4.)

8. State in your own words (prose, poetry, prayer) your understanding of the message of the cross (1:18). (See Mark 8:31-33; Phil 2:6-11; Isa 53:5-10.)

9. Compared to the worldly understanding of wisdom and power, how is the message of the cross foolishness or a stumbling block (1:23)? (See Mark 8:34; 10:43-35; 2 Cor 12:10.)

Day 4

10. Possessing little worldly status (1:26-31), how do the Christians at Corinth fit into God's plan? (See Deut 7:7-11; Jas 2:5.)

11. Compare "boasting" about ourselves to boasting in the Lord (1:30-31). (See Jer 9:23-24.)

12. Describe a life experience that caused you to depend solely on the Lord and boast of the Lord's power (1:31). (See 1 Cor 15:9-10.)

Day 5

13. Paul voluntarily admits his fear and inadequacies (2:3-4). What point is he trying to make? (See Acts 18:9-10.)

14. If the Corinthians were spiritually mature, how would their behavior show it (2:6)?

15. Are Christians today still seeking "human wisdom"(2:6-7)? What signs do you see of this in your community or parish?

Day 6

16. Describe one or two persons who "speak God's wisdom"in your everyday life (2:7). (See Col 1:28; 2:8.)

17. Paul argues that the Corinthians have the power to speak about and understand God's wisdom (2:11-16). How? When have you experienced that same power in yourself?

18. Do you ever find yourself offering God your own advice or suggesting a plan of action? How can you remind yourself to trust in the purposes and plans of God (2:16)? (See 2:5; Job 42:2-3; Rom 11:33.)

I Corinthians 3–4

NCBC-NT VOLUME 7, PAGES 28–36

Day 1

1. Share an insight from last week's study or lecture that stuck with you.

2. How can we tell that the Corinthians are still immature (3:1-4)? (See Prov 22:10; Gal 5:20.)

3. What is happening among the Corinthians to undermine God's work (3:4)?

Day 2

4. Who was Apollos and what was his ministry (3:5)? (See Acts 18:24-28.)

5. Use an example from your own experience to illustrate what Paul is trying to say in 3:6-9.

6. a) Describe a good experience of cooperation in your parish.

   b) What attitudes helped bring it about?

Day 3

7. What role should the Corinthians play in constructing God's building (3:10-13)?

8. Reflect on a gift or talent others have observed in you. How can you use it to "build on the foundation" in your parish (3:10)?

9. What does Paul mean by the "temple of God" in 3:16-17? (See John 2:21; 1 Cor 6:19; 2 Cor 6:16.)

Day 4

10. Name some current societal standards that Paul might consider "foolishness" (3:19).

11. What are some of the signs that a person is a trustworthy servant or steward (4:1-2)? (See Luke 12:42-44; 2 Tim 4:7.)

12. Why is it dangerous and futile for the Corinthians to judge ministers (4:5)?

Day 5

13. List scriptural virtues we could use to keep us from judging others. (See Zech 7:9; Matt 7:1-3; Eph 4:32; Jas 3:17-18.)

14. How do Paul's three questions serve as a "reality check" for the Corinthians (4:7)? (See John 3:27.)

15. In what circumstances do you tend to get "puffed up" about your own efforts?

Day 6

16. a) Why are the Corinthians so puffed up about themselves (4:6-8)?

    b) How do Paul and Apollos see themselves (4:9-13)?

17. Paul urges the Corinthians to imitate him. How is he their "father" (4:15-16)? (See Rom 4:18; 1 Thess 2:7.)

18. Can you identify the person(s) who "mothered" or "fathered" your own growth in faith? Describe.

First Corinthians 5–6

NCBC-NT VOLUME 7, PAGES 36–46

Day 1

1. Recall the most important thing you learned about the Corinthians or about yourself from last week's lesson.

2. Why are the Corinthians so complacent about the sin in their midst (5:1-2)? (See 1 Tim 1:19.)

3. List attitudes and practices you rely on to preserve Christian values in your life.

Day 2

4. a) What does Paul say should be done about the sexual offender (5:1-5)?

   b) What does he hope will happen as a result?

5. Paul tells the Corinthians they are allowing immorality "of a kind not found even among pagans . . . ." What is he trying to accomplish with this accusation (5:1)?

6. a) What does yeast symbolize in 5:7?

   b) How does Paul connect yeast with the Passover? (See Exod 12:17-20.)

Day 3

7. Why does Paul allow the Corinthians to associate with immoral persons outside the Christian community, but not those within the community (5:9-13)? (See Col 4:5.)

8. List some specific ways your parish influences the larger community. (See Matt 5:13-16; Heb 13:16.)

9. Have you ever tried to redirect a Christian who has drifted from the gospel path (5:11-12)? What did you do and how well did it work? (See Wis 12:2; 2 Thess 3:14-15.)

Day 4

10. What belief leads Paul to insist that the Corinthians can settle their own disputes (6:2-3)? (See Wis 3:7-8; Matt 19:28; Rev 20:4.)

11. Why is Paul so upset with the Corinthians for bringing civil lawsuits against one another (6:3-6)? (See Rom 12:17-19; 1 Thess 5:14-15.)

12. Our society does not encourage it, but what merit could be achieved by putting up with being wronged by another person (6:7)? (See Matt 5:38-42; Luke 6:29-34; Rom 12:17.)

Day 5

13. Will the sinners named in 6:9-11 be able to enter the kingdom? (See Matt 21:31.)

14. "Everything is lawful for me" is a Corinthian slogan of liberty (6:12). How have the Corinthians misinterpreted Paul's own teaching on freedom (6:12-14)? (See Gal 5:1, 13; 2 Cor 3:17.)

15. a) What do the Corinthians tend to believe about sex and sexual morality (6:12-13)?

    b) What does Paul teach (6:13-20)? (See Rom 6:12-13; 12:1.)

Day 6

16. A temple glorifies God. Reflect for a few moments on your body as a temple of the Holy Spirit. Then list three things you could do to better maintain the Holy Spirit's temple.

17. Like most freedoms, our freedom in Christ comes with responsibilities. Name the responsibilities of the Christian life you consider most fundamental.

I Corinthians 7–8

NCBC-NT VOLUME 7, PAGES 46–54

Day 1

1. What do you remember most vividly about last week's lesson?

2. According to your commentary, Paul is sometimes accused of belittling marriage (7:1-40). What is a more accurate understanding given the context?

3. What attitude toward sexual relations within marriage do you glean from Paul in 7:1-5? (See 1 Cor 11:11; Eph 5:28-30.)

Day 2

4. Does Paul think everyone should be celibate (7:7)? Explain. (See Matt 19:12 and footnote.)

5. Does Paul's understanding of Christ's plan envision separation and divorce (7:10-11)? (See Mark 10:9-12.)

6. How is the teaching on divorce different for marriages between "believers and unbelievers" (7:12-16)?

Day 3

7. The Corinthians were very interested in marriage because Greek philosophers regularly argued its merits. Name some blessings you have experienced in celibacy and/or in marriage.

8. Paul discusses circumcision in 7:18-19. But what is his broader message? (See 7:20-24; Acts 15:1-2.)

9. Recall a time in your life when you were brought face to face with what really matters in life.

Day 4

10. Paul advises his readers to remain in their present state, whether married or not. What influences Paul most in his opinions (7:25-28)?

11. Why does Paul himself prefer celibacy (7:29-40)?

12. Reflect on marriage as a vocation from God. If you are married, list ways you answer God's call in that vocation. If not married, what do you observe in others that demonstrates that marriage can be a way to answer God's call?

Day 5

13. Describe the common Corinthian social practices that lead to questions about meat sacrificed to idols (8:1).

14. What must the Corinthians consider in deciding whether or not to eat meat sacrificed to idols (8:4-12)? (See 1 Cor 12:12; Rom 15:1-2.)

15. Give an example of a situation where a morally indifferent action could cause harm or misunderstanding in family life, business, or school.

Day 6

16. Return to the start of chapter 8 where Paul says that knowledge can make us inflated with pride (8:1). How do you tend to respond to a "know-it-all?" (See 1 Cor 1:27-30.)

17. Write about someone who uses knowledge with love and respect. How has that person built up the community (8:1)? (See 2 Thess 5:11; 1 Pet 2:4-5.)

18. This week, pray for someone in your family who is weak or vulnerable.

I Corinthians 9–10

NCBC-NT VOLUME 7, PAGES 54–62

Day 1

1. Identify something from last week's lesson that made an impact on you and tell why.

2. How can Paul claim to be an apostle (9:1)? (See 15:3-10; Gal 1:1-2.)

3. List the arguments Paul uses to establish his right to financial support (9:1-12). (See Deut 25:4; Matt 10:9-10; Gal 6:6.)

Day 2

4. What reasons lie behind Paul's decision not to take payment for his ministry (9:15)? (See Luke 16:13; 2 Cor 2:17.)

5. Why might Paul have appeared "weak" to the Corinthians in this matter (9:19-23)?

6. "True freedom is manifested in the ability to adapt one's self to the needs of others" (Commentary, p. 56). How did Paul do this?

Day 3

7. Give an example from your own life of how you adapt to the needs of others in spiritual matters.

8. How does Paul bring Corinthian culture into his arguments (9:24-27)?

9. Name three disciplines you use to become a spiritual athlete (9:24-27). Which is most effective? (See Phil 3:12-14; James 1:12.)

Day 4

10. List some of the gifts the Israelites enjoyed from God (10:1-6). (See Ps 78:13-19.)

11. What lesson does Paul want the Corinthians to learn from the experience of the Hebrews (10:11)?

12. a) Name some of society's "gifts" that can lead to spiritual complacency.

    b) Have you been immune or susceptible to these?

Day 5

13. Prayerfully read 10:13. Can you share a time that God delivered you from a seemingly hopeless predicament? Was it sudden? Gradual? Joyful? Painful? Humbling?

14. For Paul, what does the eucharistic loaf symbolize (10:16-17)? (See Luke 22:19-20; 24:30-32.)

15. How can the effects of our sharing in Holy Communion be diminished (10:16-18)? And how can we assure that we express the meaning of this sharing in our lives?

Day 6

16. What is Paul saying about the effects of participating in temple banquets in 10:20-21? (See Deut 32:7.)

17. Listen carefully to the Eucharistic Prayer at Mass (or read it at home) and write what strikes you in a new way because of this week's lesson.

18. In what ways does your daily work or routine serve the glory of God (10:31)?

I Corinthians II–I2

NCBC-NT VOLUME 7, PAGES 62–75

Day I

1. Recall something from last week's reading, study, or discussion that provided a new insight for you.

2. a) Name some characteristics/behaviors you see in others that help you become a better Christian (11:1).

   b.) Name some characteristics/behaviors others could see and imitate in you to become better Christians (11:1).

3. Paul discusses liturgical conduct in 11:2-16. What rituals of the Mass are at least partially conditioned by culture?

Day 2

4. What conclusions can you draw from 11:4-5 about the roles of men and women in ministry among the believers in Corinth?

5. What understanding might have led Corinthian Christians to abandon cultural hair covering customs (11:4-10)? (See Gal 3:27-28; 2 Cor 5:16-17.)

6. There has been much discussion about the issue of "headship" in Paul's writings where he speaks of men and women (e.g., 11:8-12; Eph 5:23.) What, however, is one of the main points that is often overlooked (11:11)? (See Gal 3:27-28.)

Day 3

7. Before diving into the eucharistic abuses found in 11:17-22, describe how and where the Lord's Supper was celebrated in Paul's day.

8. What abuses are taking place as the Corinthians celebrate the Eucharist (11:17-22)?

9. a) Name parish circumstances that can cause disunity at the Eucharist today.

    b) What underlying attitudes may cause disunity in these circumstances?

Day 4

10. Paul's words in 11:23-26 are the earliest written account of the institution of the Eucharist. Read these verses slowly two or three times and imagine yourself at the Last Supper. What comes to mind as you contemplate the scene?

11. How are past, present, and future brought together in the Mass (11:26)?

12. According to Paul, each individual is given some manifestation of the Spirit. What two things must a person do to authentically employ the gifts of the Spirit (12:3, 7)?

Day 5

13. How are the Corinthians using the gifts of the Spirit (12:3)?

14. Remember a major decision you made this past year. In what ways can you see the fruits of the Spirit manifested though this decision? (See Gal 5:22-24; 1 Pet 1:5-7.)

15. What spiritual gifts do you see in those who are studying Scripture with you?

Day 6

16. To Paul, Christians are more than just a community. What is Paul's understanding of "body" (12:12-13)? (See 1 Cor 10:17; Rom 12:4-5; Col 3:15.)

17. a) Identify some harmful effects of forgetting Paul's doctrine on the Body of Christ.

    b) Which would you most like to eliminate? Why?

18. Can you identify gifts in your parish that have come from spiritual diversity (12:12-14)?

1 Corinthians 13:1–14:25

NCBC-NT VOLUME 7, PAGES 76–81

Day 1

1. What is the main issue that surfaced for you from last week's discussion or lecture?

2. Chapter 13 is a popular reading at weddings. How can Paul's challenge to love improve other relationships? Our parishes?

3. First Corinthians 13:4-6 contains eight negative statements about love. To what do these attributes correspond? (Recall what you have been studying in chapters 1–10 about the behaviors among Christians in Corinth.)

Day 2

4. List the positive characteristics of love (13:4-8). Which of them are you most able to exhibit? When and toward whom?

5. Who embodies (embodied) for you the type of love described in 13:4-7? Take some extra time to write about him/her/them.

6. Today's workplace can be full of self-interest, jealousy, and competition. How can love as Paul describes it help you (or how did it help you in the past) survive at work?

Day 3

7. Paul and the Corinthians disagree on the value of prophecy and gifts such as tongues. Explain (13:8-13).

8. In what ways has maturity and more adult thinking increased your capacity for love (13:8-12)? (See John 8:32.)

9. Paul helps his readers look forward to the time that they will "know fully" (13:12). What do you most long to know or understand fully?

Day 4

10. How does the fact that God knows you personally affect your prayer (13:12)? (See 1 John 3:2, 20.)

11. Only love lasts forever (13:13). Compare how hard you work at love to how hard you work at other goals.

12. In baptism, we are anointed with oil for the role of prophet. Recall ways you have been able to speak to others for "building up, encouragement and solace" (14:3).

Day 5

13. Speaking in tongues refers to unintelligible speech during religious ecstasy. What is Paul's opinion of this gift (14:1-12)?

14. Prophecy also was ecstatic utterance. Discuss the reasons Paul considers it the more desirable gift (14:23-25).

15. If Paul is convinced that tongues is an inferior gift, why does he wish that all had the gift (14:5), and rejoice in his own gift of tongues (14:19)?

Day 6

16. Finish this sentence two or three ways: "People appreciate my _____." How can you use these gifts to help build up the community of Christ (14:12)?

17. a) Describe the kind of liturgy you like best (style of prayer and music, environment, etc.).

    b) How does this style of worship deepen and challenge your faith?

18. When have you sensed that "God is really in your midst" (14:25)? (See Ps 139:7-12; Acts 2:28.)

I Corinthians 14:26–15:34

NCBC-NT VOLUME 7, PAGES 81–88

Day 1

1. What is one insight that has remained with you from last week's lesson? Why?

2. a) Would the "assembly" at Corinth have resembled our Sunday liturgy (14:26)?

   b) How was the gift of tongues being misused in the assembly?

3. List the three controls Paul sets for the use of tongues (14:27-28).

Day 2

4. Why does Paul need to remind the Corinthians that God is "not the God of disorder but of peace" (14:33)? (See 14:37-40.)

5. We experience prophecy today mainly through the Liturgy of the Word. Recall and describe a homily that made a deep impact on you.

6. If you were asked to give a homily on last week's gospel, what would you say to build up, encourage, and bring solace to your listeners (14:3)? (See 2 Tim 4:1-2.)

Day 3

7. Paul's words in 14:34-35 seem to contradict his view of women's roles in 11:5, 11-12, and in other of his writings (e.g., Gal 3:28). Based on Bible footnotes and your commentary, discuss this contradiction.

8. a) What main points in the Christian gospel tradition does Paul quote (15:3-5)? (See Acts 10:36-41.)

   b) Why does Paul quote this early creed?

9. Who was Cephas (also Kephas) and what was his role among the Twelve (15:5)? (See Matt 16:13-20; Mark 3:16; 9:2-8; Gal 1:18.)

Day 4

10. a) Under what circumstances did Christ appear to Paul (15:8)? (See Acts 22:4-10.)

    b) How would you describe your own conversion to Christ? Ordinary? Extraordinary? Gradual? Explain.

11. Why does Paul call himself the "least of the apostles" (15:9)? (See Gal 1:13-23.)

12. Conventional wisdom never would have chosen Paul as a Christian apostle, but God's grace made him effective (15:10). Describe your own experience of this irony.

Day 5

13. If Corinthians deny the resurrection of the dead, their faith is useless (15:12-17). Briefly summarize Paul's argument.

14. What would the Corinthians have understood from Paul's reference to "first fruits" (15:20)?

15. Meditate a few moments on Jesus' resurrection as the assurance of your own future life. What came to mind as you reflected on this assurance?

Day 6

16. When will our resurrection take place (15:22-23)? (See John 5:28-29; 1 Thess 4:15-18.)

17. a) What does it mean to be "baptized for the dead" (15:29)?

    b) Why does Paul bring it up?

18. Paul suffers and even risks his life for the sake of the Gospel. Recall a time in your own life that your faith in Jesus caused you to suffer.

I Corinthians 15:35–16:24

NCBC-NT VOLUME 7, PAGES 88–95

Day 1

1. What would you choose to reemphasize from last week's lesson?

2. The Corinthians want to know what a resurrected body will look like. How does Paul explain it (15:35-44)?

3. Refer to the following biblical seed metaphors. Then relate a real-life experience where you had to "die"to something in order to experience new growth. (See Ps 126:4-6; Matt 13:1-10; John 12:24-25).

Day 2

4. Name some weaknesses of the present human condition that you will be happy to be rid of in your "glorified"body (15:42-22). (See 2:9.)

5. What is your understanding of 15:45-49?

6. In what life circumstances might 15:58 be comforting to a believer? (See 2 Cor 4:16-18; Gal 5:6.)

Day 3

7. Why should the Gentile Christians contribute to a collection for the Jewish Christians in Jerusalem (16:1-4)? (See Rom 15:25-27; Gal 2:1-10.)

8. Which church collection do you consider most important? Why?

9. Who was Apollos, and were Paul and Apollos rivals (16:12)? (See 3:5-9; Acts 18:24-28.)

Day 4

10. What were Paul's travel plans (16:5-9)?

11. Why does Paul fear that Timothy might be treated poorly (16:10-11)? (See 1 Tim 4:12; 2 Tim 1:6-8.)

12. a) Which model members of the Corinthian community does Paul single out (16:15-18)?

    b) What makes them models?

Day 5

13. Paul ends his letter by reinforcing that *all* believers are part of a new family of faith. Make plans now to reach out to a fellow believer who is "different" from you. Describe your plan.

14. First Corinthians greatly forms our understanding of the Eucharist (11:17-33.) What was most significant to you in this part of the lesson?

15. First Corinthians 13:4-7 is a familiar and well-loved New Testament passage. Write your own "hymn of love." List concrete ways to love well in your current life circumstances.

Day 6

16. Even after almost 2000 years, we face many of the same challenges the Corinthians did. What parts of 1 Corinthians make you feel most hopeful as we move into the future?

17. Our goal in reading and studying the Bible is always to become closer to Christ. Reflect on ways that has happened during this study. What contributed most to your growth?

NOTES